A STORY OF ANTI-CHRIST

VLADIMIR SERGAEVITCH SOLOVIEV

ISBN: 1475136838
ISBN-13: 978-1475136838

First Published 1900.

2012 Reprint By Kassock Bros. Publishing Co.

VLADIMIR SERGAEVITCH SOLOVIEV

1853 - 1900

He can be explained by a simple proverb.

"All that glitters is not gold."

A SHORT STORY OF THE ANTI-CHRIST

Pan-Mongolism! The name is wild,
Yet it pleases my ear greatly,
As if it were full of forebodings
Of the great destiny appointed by God. . . .

LADY - Where does this motto come from?

MR. Z - I think it is the work of the author himself.

LADY - Well, we are listening.

MR. Z - *(reads).* The twentieth century was the epoch of the last great wars and revolutions. The greatest of these wars had its distant cause in the movement of *Pan Mongolism* which originated in Japan as far back as the end of the nineteenth century. The imitative Japanese, who showed such wonderful speed and success in copying the external forms of European culture, also assimilated certain European ideas of the baser sort. Having learned from newspapers and textbooks on history that there were in the West such movements as Pan-Hellenism, Pan-Germanism, Pan-Slavism, and Pan-Islamism, they proclaimed to the world the great idea of Pan-Mongolism - the unification under their leadership of all the races of Eastern Asia, with the aim of conducting a decisive war against foreign intruders, that is, against the Europeans.

Taking advantage of the fact that at the beginning of the twentieth century Europe was engaged in a final decisive struggle against the Moslem world, they seized the opportunity to attempt the reaction of their great plan - first, by occupying Korea, then Peking, where, assisted by the revolutionary party in China, they deposed the old Manchu dynasty and put in its place a Japanese one. In this the Chinese Conservatives soon acquiesced, as they understood that, of two evils, the lesser is the better, and that "family ties make all people brothers, whether they wish it or not."

The independence of old China as a state had already proved unable to maintain itself, and subjection to the Europeans or the Japanese became inevitable. It seemed clear that the dominance of the Japanese, though it abolished the external forms of the Chinese state organization (which anyway had become palpably worthless), would not interfere with the main foundations of national life, whereas the dominance of the European Powers, which for political reasons supported the Christian missionaries, threatened the very spiritual basis of China. The national hatred in which the Japanese were formerly held by the Chinese had developed at a time when neither one nor the other knew the Europeans, and consequently this enmity of two kindred nations acquired the character of a family feud and was as unreasonable as it was ridiculous.

The Europeans, however, were *unreservedly* alien, nothing but enemies, and their predominance promised nothing that could flatter national ambition, while in the hands of Japan the Chinese saw the delightful lure of Pan-Mongolism which, at the same time, was more acceptable to their minds than the painful necessity of assimilating the external forms of the European culture.

"Will you understand, you obstinate brothers," the Japanese repeatedly urged them, "that we take weapons from the Western dogs, not because we like them, but simply to beat them with their own devices? If you join us and accept our practical guidance, we shall soon be able not only to drive out all the white devils from our Asia but, also, to conquer their own lands and establish the true Middle Kingdom over the whole world. You are right in your national pride and your contempt for the Europeans but you should nourish these feelings, not only with dreams but with sensible actions as well. In these latter, we Japanese are far in advance of you and have to show you the ways of mutual benefit. If you look around, you will see yourselves what little gains you have obtained by your policy of confidence in yourselves and mistrust of us, your natural friends and protectors. You have seen how Russia and England, Germany and France nearly divided you up among themselves, and how all your tigerish schemes could show only the harmless end of the serpent's tail."

The sensible Chinese found this argument reasonable, and the Japanese dynasty became firmly established. Its first care was, of course, to create a powerful army and fleet. The greater part of the Japanese troops were brought over to China and served as a nucleus for the new colossal army. The Japanese officers who could speak Chinese proved much more successful instructors than the dismissed Europeans, while the immense population of China, with Manchuria, Mongolia, and Tibet, provided a sufficient supply of good fighting material.

It was already possible for the first Emperor of the Japanese dynasty to make a successful test of the power of the new Empire by driving out the French from Tonkin and Siam, the English from Burma, and then by adding the whole of Indochina to the Middle Kingdom.

His successor, the second Emperor, Chinese on his mother's side, combined in himself Chinese cunning and tenacity with Japanese energy, agility, and enterprise. He mobilized an army four million strong in Chinese Turkestan, and while Tsun-li-Yamin was confidentially informing the Russian Ambassador that this army was intended for the invasion of India, the Emperor with his immense forces suddenly invaded Russian Central Asia. Here, having raised against us all the population, he rapidly crossed the Ural Mountains, overrunning Eastern and Central Russia with his troops.

Meanwhile, the Russian armies, mobilized in all haste, were hurrying to meet them from Poland and Lithuania, Kiev and Volhyn, St. Petersburg, and Finland. Having no ready plan of campaign, and being faced with an immense superiority in numbers, the fighting qualities of the Russian armies were sufficient only to allow them to perish with honor.

The swiftness of the invasion left them no time for a proper concentration, and army corps after army corps were annihilated in desperate and hopeless battles. The Mongolian victories also involved huge losses, but these were easily made good with the help of the many Asiatic railways, while the Russian army, two hundred thousand strong and for some time concentrated on the Manchurian frontier, made an abortive attempt to invade well-defended China.

After leaving a portion of his forces in Russia, so that no new armies could form in that country - and also in order to fight the numerous bodies of partisan units - the Emperor crossed the frontiers of Germany with three armies. In this case the country had had sufficient time to prepare itself, and one of the Mongolian armies met with a crushing defeat. At this time, the party of a belated *revanche* was in power in France, and soon the Germans found an army of a million bayonets in their rear.

Finding itself between the hammer and the anvil, the German army was compelled to accept the honorable terms of peace offered to it by the Chinese Emperor. The exultant French, fraternizing with the yellow faces, scattered over Germany and soon lost all notion of military discipline. The Emperor ordered his army to kill any allies who were no longer useful and, with Chinese punctiliousness, the order was executed with precision.

Simultaneously, in Paris, workers *sans patrie*[1] organized an uprising and the capital of Western culture joyfully opened its gates to the Lord of the East. His curiosity satisfied, the Emperor set off to Boulogne where, protected by the fleet that had come round from the Pacific, transports were speedily prepared for ferrying his army over to England.

1 Without state or nation.

The Emperor was in need of money, however, and so the English succeeded in buying him off with the sum of one million pounds. Within a year, all the European States submitted as vassals to the domination of the Chinese Emperor, who, having left sufficient occupation troops in Europe, returned to the East in order to organize naval expeditions against America and Australia.

The new Mongolian yoke over Europe lasted for half a century. The domain of the inner life of thought of this epoch was marked by a general blending and mutual interchange of European and Eastern ideas, providing a repetition on a grand scale of ancient Alexandrian syncretism.

In the practical domain, three phenomena above all were most characteristic: the great influx into Europe of Chinese and Japanese workers and the consequent acuteness of social and economic problems; the continued activity of the ruling classes in the way of palliative attempts in order to solve those problems; and, lastly, the increased activity of secret international societies, organizing a great European conspiracy for expelling the Mongols and reestablishing the independence of Europe.

This colossal conspiracy, which was supported by local national governments, insofar as they could evade the control of the Emperor's viceroys, was organized in masterly fashion and was crowned with most brilliant success. An appointed hour saw the beginning of a massacre of the Mongolian soldiers and of the annihilation and expulsion of the Asiatic workers. Secret cadres of European troops were suddenly revealed in various places, and a general mobilization was carried out according to plans previously prepared.

The new Emperor, who was a grandson of the great conqueror, rushed from China to Russia, but his innumerable hordes suffered a crushing defeat at the hands of the All-European Army. Their scattered remnants returned to the interior of Asia, and Europe breathed freely again. If the half-century of submission to the Asiatic barbarians was due to the disunity of the European States which had concerned themselves only with their own national interests, a great and glorious independence was achieved by an international organization of the united forces of the entire European population.

As a natural consequence of this fact, the old traditional organization of individual States was everywhere deprived of its former importance, and the last traces of ancient monarchal institutions gradually disappeared. Europe in the twenty-first century represented an alliance of more or less democratic nations - the United States of Europe. The progress of material culture, somewhat interrupted by the Mongolian yoke and the war of liberation, now burst forth with a greater force.

The problems of inner consciousness, however, such as the questions of life and death, the ultimate destiny of the world and humanity, made more complicated and involved by the latest researches and discoveries in the fields of psychology and physiology these as before remained unsolved. Only one important, though negative, result made itself apparent. This was the final bankruptcy of the materialistic theory. The notion of the universe as a system of dancing atoms, and of life as the result of mechanical accumulation of the slightest changes in material no longer satisfied a single reasoning intellect.

Humanity had outgrown that stage *of philosophical infancy.* On the other hand, it became equally evident that it had also outgrown the infantile capacity for naive, unconscious faith. Such ideas as God creating the universe out of nothing were no longer taught even in elementary schools. A certain high level of ideas concerning such subjects had been evolved, and no dogmatism could risk a descent below it. And though the majority of thinking people had remained faithless, the few believers, of necessity, had become thinking, thus fulfilling the commandment of the Apostle: "Be infants in your hearts, but not in your reason[2]."

At that time, there was among the few believing spiritualists a remarkable person - many called him a superman - who was equally far from both, intellect and childlike heart. He was still young, but owing to his great genius, by the age of thirty-three he had already become famous as a great thinker, writer, and public figure. Conscious of the great power of spirit in himself, he was always a confirmed spiritualist, and his clear intellect always showed him the truth of what one should believe in: the good, God, and the Messiah.

In these he believed, but he loved only himself. He believed in God, but in the depths of his soul he involuntarily and unconsciously preferred himself. He believed in Good, but the All Seeing Eye of the Eternal knew that this man would bow down before the power of Evil as soon as it would offer him a bribe - not by deception of the senses and the lower passions, not even by the superior bait of power, but only by his own immeasurable self-love.

This self-love was neither an unconscious instinct nor an insane ambition. Apart from his exceptional genius, beauty, and nobility of character, the reserve, disinterestedness, and active sympathy with those in need which he evinced to such a great extent seemed abundantly to justify the immense self-love of this great spiritualist, ascetic, and philanthropist. Did he deserve blame because, being as he was so generously supplied with the gifts of God, he saw in them the signs of Heaven's special benevolence to him, and thought himself to be second only to God himself? In a word, he considered himself to be what Christ in reality was. But this conception of his higher value showed itself in practice not in the exercise of his moral duty to God and the world but in seizing his privilege and advantage at the expense of others, and of Christ in particular.

---

2 1 Corinthians 14:20.

At first, he bore no ill feeling toward Christ. He recognized his messianic importance and value, but he was sincere in seeing in him only his own greatest precursor. The moral achievement of Christ and his uniqueness were beyond an intellect so completely clouded by self-love as his. Thus he reasoned: "Christ came before me. I come second. But what, in order of time, appears later is, in its essence, of greater importance. I come last, at the end of history, and for the very reason that I am most perfect. I am the final savior of the world, and Christ is my precursor. His mission was to precede and prepare for my coming."

Thinking thus, the superman of the twenty-first century applied to himself everything that was said in the Gospels about the second coming, explaining the latter not as a return of the same Christ, but as a replacing of the preliminary Christ by the final one - that is, by himself.

At this stage, the coming man presented few original characteristics or features. His attitude toward Christ resembled, for instance, that of Mohammed, a truthful man, against whom no charge of harboring evil designs can be brought.

This man justified his selfish preference of himself before Christ in yet another way. 'Christ,' he said, "who preached and practiced moral good in life, was a *reformer* of humanity, whereas I am called to be the *benefactor* of that same humanity, partly reformed and partly incapable of being reformed. I will give everyone what they require. As a moralist, Christ divided humanity by the notion of good and evil. I shall unite it by benefits which are as much needed by good as by evil people. I shall be the true representative of that God who makes his sun to shine upon the good and the evil alike, and who makes the rain to fall upon the just and the unjust. Christ brought the sword; I shall bring peace. Christ threatened the earth with the Day of Judgment. But I shall be the last judge, and my judgment will be not only that of justice but also that of mercy. The justice that will be meted out in my sentences will not be a retributive justice but a distributive one. I shall judge each person according to his deserts, and shall give everybody what he needs."

In this magnificent spirit he now waited for God to call him in some unmistakable way to take upon himself the work of saving humanity - for some obvious and striking testimony that he was the elder son, the beloved first-born child of God. He waited and sustained himself by the consciousness of his superhuman virtues and gifts, for, as was said, he was a man of irreproachable morals and exceptional genius.

Thus this just, proud man awaited the sanction of the Most High in order to begin his saving of humanity; but he saw no signs of it. He had passed the age of thirty. Three more years passed. Suddenly, a thought leaped into his mind and thrilled him to the core. "What," he thought, "what if by some accident it is not I, but the other ... the Galilean. What if he is not my annunciator but the true deliverer, the first and the last? In that case, he must be *alive*... But where is he, then? What if he suddenly comes to me... here, now? What shall I tell Him? Shall I not be compelled to kneel down before him as the very last silly Christian, as some Russian peasant who mutters without understanding: 'Lord, Jesus Christ, forgive me, a sinful man'? Shall I not be compelled like an old Polish woman to prostrate myself? I, the serene genius, the superman! It cannot be!"

And here, instead of his former reasoning and cold reverence to God and Christ, a sudden fear was born and grew in his heart, next followed by a burning *envy* that consumed all his being, and by an ardent hatred that took his very breath away. "It is I, it is I, and not he! He is dead - is and will ever be! He did not - no, did not rise! He is rotting in the grave, rotting as the lost..." His mouth foaming, he rushed convulsively out of the house, through the garden, and ran along a rocky path into the silent black night.

His rage calmed down and gave place to a despair, dry and heavy as the rocks, somber as the night. He stopped in front of a sharp precipice, from the bottom of which he could hear the faint sounds of the stream running over the stones. An unbearable anguish pressed upon his heart. Suddenly a thought flashed across his mind. "Shall I call him? Shall I ask him what to do?" And in the midst of darkness he could see a pale and grief-stained image. "He pities me ... Oh, no, never! He did not rise! He did not! He did not!" And he leapt from the precipice.

But something firm like a column of water held him up in the air. He felt a shock as if of electricity, and some unknown force hurled him back. For a moment he became unconscious. When he came to his senses he found himself kneeling down a few paces from the brow of the precipice. A strange figure gleaming with a dim phosphorescent light loomed up before him, and its two eyes pierced his soul with their painful penetrating glitter...

He saw these two piercing eyes and heard some unfamiliar voice coming from inside or outside him - he could not tell which - a dull, muffled voice, yet distinct, metallic, and expressionless as a recording. And the voice said to him: "Oh, my beloved son! Let all my benevolence rest on thee! Why didst not thou seek for me? Why hast thou stooped to worship that other, the bad one, and his father? I am thy god and father. And that crucified beggar - he is a stranger both to me and to thee. I have no other son but thee. Thou art the sole, the only begotten, the equal of myself. I love thee, and ask for nothing from thee. Thou art so beautiful, great, and mighty. Do thy work in *thine own* name, not mine. I harbor no envy of thee. I love thee. I require nothing of thee. He whom thou regardest as God, demanded of his son obedience, absolute obedience - even to death on a cross - and even there he did not help Him. I demand nothing of thee, and I will help thee. For the sake of thyself, for the sake of thine own dignity and excellency, and for the sake of my own disinterested love of thee, I will help thee! Receive thou my spirit! As before my spirit gave birth to thee in *beauty, so* now it gives birth to thee in *power."*

With these words, the superman's mouth opened involuntarily, two piercing eyes came close to his face, and he felt an icy breath which pervaded the whole of his being. He felt in himself such strength, vigor, lightness, and joy as he had never before experienced. At that moment, the luminous image and the two eyes suddenly disappeared, and something lifted the man into the air and brought him down in his own garden before the very doors of his house.

Next day, the visitors of the great man, and even his servants, were startled by his special inspired air. They would have been even more startled could they have seen with what supernatural quickness and facility he was writing, locked up in his study, his famous work entitled *The Open Way to Universal Peace and Prosperity.*

The superman's previous books and public activity had always met with severe criticism, though these came chiefly from people of exceptionally deep religious convictions, who for that very reason possessed no authority (I am, after all, speaking of the coming of the Anti-Christ) and thus they were hardly listened to when they tried to point out, in everything that the "coming man" wrote or said, the signs of a quite exceptional and excessive self-love and conceit, and a complete absence of true simplicity, frankness, and sincerity.

But now, with his new book, he brought over to his side even some of his former critics and adversaries. This book, composed after the incident at the precipice, evinced a greater power of genius than he had ever shown before. it was a work that embraced everything and solved every problem. It united a noble respect for ancient traditions and symbols with a broad and daring radicalism in socio-political questions. It joined a boundless freedom of thought with the most profound appreciation for everything mystical. Absolute individualism stood side by side with an ardent zeal for the common good, and the highest idealism in guiding principles combined smoothly with a perfect definiteness in practical solutions for the necessities of life. And all this was blended and cemented with such artistic genius that every thinker and every man of action, however one-sided he might have been, could easily view and accept the whole from his particular individual standpoint without sacrificing anything to the *truth itself,* without actually rising above his *ego,* without *in reality* renouncing his one-sidedness, without correcting the inadequacy of his views and wishes, and without making up their deficiencies.

This wonderful book was immediately translated into the languages of all the civilized nations, and many of the uncivilized ones as well. During the entire year thousands of newspapers in all parts of the world were filled with the publisher's advertisements and the critics' praises. Cheap editions with portraits of the author were sold in millions of copies, and all the civilized world - which now stood for nearly all the globe resounded with the glory of the incomparable, the great, the only one!

Nobody raised his voice against the book. On every side it was accepted by all as the revelation of the complete truth. In it, all the past was given such full and due justice, the present was appraised with such impartiality and catholicity, and the happiest future was described in such a convincing and practical manner that everybody could not help saying: "Here at last we have what we need. Here is the ideal, which is not a Utopia. Here is a scheme which is not a dream." And the wonderful author not only impressed all, but he was *agreeable* to all, so that the word of Christ was fulfilled: "I have come in the name of the Father, and you accept me not. *Another* will come in *his own* name - him you *will* accept." For it is necessary to be *agreeable* to be *accepted.*

It is true some pious people, while praising the book wholeheartedly, had been asking why the name of Christ was never mentioned in it; but other Christians had rejoined: "So much the better. Everything sacred has already been stained enough in past ages by every sort of unacknowledged zealot, and nowadays a deeply religious author must be extremely guarded in these matters. Since the book is imbued with the true Christian spirit of active love and all-embracing goodwill, what more do you want?" And everybody agreed.

Soon after the publication of *The Open Way*, which made its author the most popular man ever to live on earth, an international constitutional congress of the United States of Europe was to be held in Berlin. This Union, founded after a series of international and civil wars which had been brought about by the liberation from the Mongolian yoke and had resulted in considerable alteration in the map of Europe, was now menaced with peril, not through conflicts of nations but through the internal strife between various political and social parties.

The principal directors of European policy, who belonged to the powerful brotherhood of Freemasons, felt the lack of a common executive power. The European unity that had been obtained at so great a cost was every moment threatening to fall to pieces. There was no unanimity in the Union Council or *Comité permanent universel*[3], for not all the seats were in the hands of true Masons.

The independent members of the Council were entering into separate agreements, and this state of affairs threatened another war. The "initiated" then decided to establish a one-man executive power endowed with some considerable authority. The principal candidate was the secret member of the Order - "the Coming Man." He was the only man with a great worldwide fame. Being by profession a learned artilleryman, and by his source of income a rich capitalist, he was on friendly terms with many in financial and military circles. In another, less enlightened time, there might have been held against him the fact of his extremely obscure origin. His mother, a lady of doubtful reputation, was very well known in both hemispheres, but the number of people who had grounds to

3 Standing universal committee.

consider him as their son was rather too great. These circumstances, however, could not carry any weight with an age that was so advanced as to be actually the last. "The Coming Man" was almost unanimously elected president of the United States of Europe for life. And when he appeared on the platform in all the glamor of youthful superhuman beauty and power and, with inspired eloquence, expounded his universal program, the assembly was carried away by the spell of his personality and, in an outburst of enthusiasm, decided, even without voting, to give him the highest honor and to elect him Roman Emperor.

The congress closed amid general rejoicing, and the great man who had been chosen published a manifesto which began with the words: "Nations of the World! I give you my peace," and concluded, "Nations of the World! The promises have been fulfilled! An eternal universal peace has been secured. Every attempt to destroy it will meet with determined and irresistible opposition, since a middle power is now established on earth which is stronger than all the other powers, separately or conjointly. This unconquerable, all-surmountable power belongs to me, the authorized chosen one of Europe, the Emperor of all its forces. International law has at last secured the sanction which was so long missing. Henceforth, no Power will dare to say 'War' when I say 'Peace!' Peoples of the world, peace to you!"

This manifesto had the desired effect. Everywhere outside Europe, particularly in America, powerful imperialist parties were formed which compelled their governments to join the United States of Europe under the supreme authority of the Roman Emperor.

There still remained a few independent tribes and little states in remote parts of Asia and Africa but, with a small but chosen army of Russian, German, Polish, Hungarian, and Turkish regiments, the Emperor set out for a military march from East Asia to Morocco and, without much bloodshed, brought into subjection all the insubordinate States. In all the countries of the two hemispheres, he installed his viceroys, choosing them from among the native nobility who had received a European education and were faithful to him. In all the heathen countries, the native populations, greatly impressed and charmed by his personality, proclaimed him as their supreme god.

In a single year, a real universal monarchy in the true and proper sense of the word was established. The germs of wars were radically destroyed. The Universal League of Peace met for the last time, and having delivered an exalted panegyric to the Great Peacemaker, dissolved itself as being no longer necessary.

On the eve of the second year of his reign, the World's Emperor published a new manifesto: 'Nations of the World! I have promised you peace, and I have given it to you. But peace is joyful only through prosperity. Who in peacetime is threatened with poverty has no pleasure in peace. I call, therefore, all the cold and hungry ones to come to me, and I will give you food and warmth!"

Here he announced the simple and comprehensive program of social reform that had already been articulated in his book and which now captured all noble and sound minds. Owing to the concentration in his hands of all the financial resources of the world and all its colossal land properties, the Emperor could carry into effect his reform in accordance with the wishes of the poor and without causing much pain to the rich. All now received according to their capabilities, and every capability according to its labors and merits.

The new lord of the world was above all else a kindhearted philanthropist and not only a philanthropist, but even a *philozoist,* a lover of life. He was a vegetarian himself, prohibited vivisection, and instituted strict supervision over the slaughter-houses; while societies for the protection of animals received from him every encouragement.

But what was more important than these details, the most fundamental form of equality was firmly established among humankind, the *equality of universal satiety.* This took place in the second year of his reign. Social and economic problems finally had been settled. But if satisfaction is a question of primary importance for the hungry, the satisfied ones crave for something else. Even satiated animals usually want not only to sleep but also to play - the more so with humanity which has always *post panem* craved for *circenses*[4].

The Emperor Superman understood what his mob wanted. At that time a great magician, enwrapped in a dense cloud of strange facts and wild stories, came to him in Rome from the Far East. A rumor, spreading among the neo-Buddhists, credited him with a divine origin from the sun god Suria and some river nymph.

This magician, Apollonius by name, was doubtless a person of genius. A semi-Asiatic and a semi-European, a Catholic bishop *in partibus infidelium*[5], he combined in himself in a most striking manner knowledge of the latest conclusions and applications of Western science with the art of utilizing all that was really sound and important in traditional Eastern mysticism. The results of this combination were startling. Apollonius learned, among other things, the semi-scientific, semi-mystic art of attracting and directing at will atmospheric electricity and the people said of him that he could *bring down fire from heaven.* However, though he was able to startle the imagination of the crowd by various unheard-of phenomena, for some time he did not abuse his power for any special or selfish ends.

It was this man who came to the great Emperor, saluted him as the true son of God, declaring that he had discovered in the secret

4 "Bread and circuses" from the Latin *"panem et circenses"* is a metaphor for a superficial means of appeasement.

5 Latin, "in the lands of unbelievers." Words once added to the name of many of the sees conferred on non-residential or titular Roman Catholic bishops.

books of the East certain unmistakable prophecies pointing to the Emperor as the last savior and judge of the Universe, and offering him his services and all his art. The Emperor, completely charmed by the man, accepted him as a gift from above, decorated him with all kinds of gorgeous titles, and made him his constant companion. So the nations of the world, after they had received from their lord universal peace and universal abolition of hunger, were now given the possibility of never-ending enjoyment of most diverse and extraordinary miracles. Thus came to end the third year of the reign of the superman.

After this happy solution of political and social problems, the religious question came to the fore. The question was raised by the Emperor himself, in the first place, in its application to Christianity. At the time, the situation of Christianity was as follows: Its followers had greatly diminished in numbers and barely included forty-five million people in the whole world; but, morally, it had made a marked progress and had gained in quality what it had lost in numbers. People who were not bound to Christianity by any spiritual tie were no longer counted as Christians.

The various Christian persuasions had diminished fairly equally in their numbers, so that the proportional relationship among them remained almost unchanged. As to mutual feelings, hostility had not entirely given place to amity but had considerably softened down, and points of disagreement had lost much of their former acuteness. The Papacy had long before been expelled from Rome, and after long wanderings had found refuge in St. Petersburg on condition that it refrain from propaganda there and in the country.

In Russia, the Papacy soon became greatly simplified. Leaving practically unchanged the number of its colleges and offices, it was obliged to infuse into their work a more fervent spirit, and to reduce to the smallest limits its elaborate rituals and ceremonials. Many strange and seductive customs, though not formally abolished, fell of themselves into disuse. In all the other countries, particularly in

North America, the Catholic priesthood still had a good many representatives possessed of strong will, inexhaustible energy, and independent character, who welded together the Catholic Church into a closer unity than it had ever seen before, and who preserved for it its international, cosmopolitan importance.

As to Protestantism, which was still led by Germany, especially since the union of the greater part of the Anglican Church with the Catholic one - Protestantism had purged itself of its extreme negative tendencies, and the supporters of these tendencies openly descended into religious apathy and unbelief. The Evangelical Church now contained only the sincerely religious. It was headed by people who combined a vast learning with a deep religious feeling and an ever-growing desire to bring to life again in their own persons the living image of the true ancient Christianity.

Russian Orthodoxy, after political events had altered the official position of the Church, lost many millions of its sham and nominal members; but it won the joy of unification with the best part of the "old believers," and even many of the deeply religious sectarians. The revivified Church, though not increasing in numbers, began to grow in strength of spirit, which it particularly revealed in its struggle with the numerous extremist sects (some not entirely devoid of the demoniacal and satanic element) which found root among the people and in society.

During the first two years of the new reign, all Christians, frightened and weary of the number of preceding revolutions and wars, looked upon their new lord and his peaceful reforms partly with benevolent expectation and partly with unreserved sympathy and even fervent enthusiasm.

But in the third year, after the great magician had made his appearance, serious fears and antipathy began to grow in the minds of many an Orthodox, Catholic and Protestant. The Gospel and Apostolic texts speaking of the Prince of this Age and of the Anti-

Christ were now read more carefully and led to lively comments. The Emperor soon perceived from certain signs that a storm was brewing, and he resolved to bring the matter to a head without any further delay. In the beginning of the fourth year of his reign, he published a manifesto to all true Christians, without distinction of churches, inviting them to elect or appoint authoritative representatives for the world congress to be held under his presidency.

At that time, the imperial residence was transferred from Rome to Jerusalem. Palestine was already an autonomous province, inhabited and governed mainly by the Jews. Jerusalem was a free and now imperial city. The Christian shrines remained unmolested but, over the whole of the large platform of Haram-esh-Sheriff, extending from Birket-Israin and the barracks right to the mosque of El-Ax and "Solomon's Stables," an immense building was erected, incorporating in itself, besides the two small ancient mosques, a huge "Empire" temple for the unification of all cults, and two luxurious imperial palaces with libraries, museums, and special apartments for magical experiments and exercises.

It was in this half-temple, half-palace that the world congress was to meet on September 14th. As the Evangelical Church has no hierarchy in the proper sense of the word, the Catholic and Orthodox hierarchy, in compliance with the express wish of the Emperor, and in order that a greater uniformity of representation should obtain, decided to admit to the proceedings of the congress a certain number of lay members known for their piety and devotion to Church interests. Once, however, these were admitted, it seemed impossible to exclude from the congress the clergy, of both monastic and secular orders. In this way the total number of members at the congress exceeded three thousand, while about half a million Christian pilgrims flooded Jerusalem and all Palestine.

Among the members present, three men were particularly conspicuous. The first was Pope Peter II, who legitimately led the

Catholic part of the congress. His predecessor had died on the way to the congress, and a conclave had met in Damascus, and unanimously elected Cardinal Simone Barionini, who took the name of Peter. He came of plebeian stock, from the province of Naples, and had become famous as a preacher of the Carmelite Order, having earned great successes in fighting a certain Satanic sect which was spreading in St. Petersburg and its environs and seducing not only the Orthodox but the Catholic faithful as well.

Raised to the archbishopric of Mogilov and next to the Cardinal's chair, he was all along marked for the tiara. He was a man of fifty, of middle stature and strongly built, with a red face, a crooked nose, and thick eyebrows. He had an impulsive and ardent temperament, spoke with fervor and with sweeping gestures, and enthused more than convinced his audience. The new Pope had no trust in the Emperor, and looked at him with a disapproving eye, particularly since the deceased Pope, yielding to the Emperor's pressure, had made a cardinal of the Imperial Chancellor and great magician of the world, the exotic Bishop Apollonius, whom Peter regarded as a doubtful Catholic and a certain fraud.

The actual, though not official, leader of the Orthodox members was the Elder John, extremely well known among the Russian people. Officially, he was considered a bishop "in retirement," but he did not live in any monastery, being always engaged in traveling all over the world. Many legendary stories were circulated about him. Some people believed that he was Feodor Kuzmich, that is, Emperor Alexander I, who had died three centuries back and was now raised to life. Others went further and maintained that he was the true Elder John, that is, John the Apostle, who had never died and had now openly reappeared in the latter days. He himself said nothing about his origin and younger days. He was now a very old but vigorous man with white hair and a beard tinged with a yellowish, even greenish color, tall, thin in body, with full, slightly rosy cheeks, vivid sparkling eyes and a tender, kind expression in his face and speech. He was always dressed in a white cassock and mantle.

Heading the Evangelical members of the congress was the very learned German theologian, Professor Ernst Pauli. He was a short, wizened old man, with a huge forehead, sharp nose, and a cleanly shaven chin. His eyes were distinguished by their peculiarly ferocious and yet kindly gaze. He incessantly rubbed his hands, shook his head, sternly knitted his brows and pursed up his lips; while with eyes all flashing he sternly ejaculated: "So! Nun! Ja! So also!" His dress bore all the appearance of solemnity - a white tie and long pastoral frock coat decorated with signs of his order.

The opening of the congress was most imposing. Two thirds of the immense temple, devoted to the "unification of all cults," was covered with benches and other seating arrangements for members of the congress. The remaining third was taken up by a high platform on which were placed the Emperor's throne and another, lesser throne a little below it intended for the great magician - who was at the same time cardinal and imperial chancellor - and behind them rows of armchairs for the ministers, courtiers, and State officials, while along the side there were still longer rows of armchairs, the intended occupants of which remained undisclosed.

The gallery was taken by the orchestra, while in the adjoining square there were installed two regiments of Guards and a battery of guns for triumphal salvos. The members of the congress had already attended their respective services in their various churches: the opening of the congress was to be entirely civil. When the Emperor, accompanied by the great magician and his suite, made his entrance, the band began to play the "March of Unified Humanity," which was the international hymn of the Empire, and all the members rose to their feet, and, waving their hats, gave three enthusiastic cheers: "Vivat! Hurrah! Hoch!"

The Emperor, standing by the throne and stretching forward his hand with an air of majestic benevolence, proclaimed in a sonorous and pleasing voice: "Christians of all sects! My beloved subjects, brothers and sisters! From the beginning of my reign, which the Most High blessed with such wonderful and glorious deeds, I have had no cause to be dissatisfied with you. You have always performed your duties true to your faith and conscience. But this is not enough for me. My sincere love for you, my beloved brothers and sisters, thirsts for reciprocation. I wish you to recognize in me your true leader in every enterprise undertaken for the well-being of humanity, not merely out of your sense of duty to me but mainly out of your heartfelt love for me. So now, besides what I generally do for all, I am about to show you my special benevolence. Christians! What can I bestow upon you? What can I give you, not as my subjects, but as my co-religionists, my brothers and sisters! Christians! Tell me what is the most precious thing for you in Christianity, so that I may direct my efforts to that end?"

He stopped for a moment, waiting for an answer. The hall was filled with reverberating muffled sounds. The members of the congress were consulting each other. Pope Peter, with fervent gestures, was explaining something to his followers. Professor Pauli was shaking his head and ferociously smacking his lips. The Elder John, bending over Eastern bishops and monks quietly tried to impress something upon them.

After he had waited a few minutes, the Emperor again addressed the congress in the same kind tone, in which, however, there could be heard a scarcely perceptible note of irony: "Dear Christians," he said, "I understand how difficult it is for you to give me a direct answer. I will help you also in this. From time immemorial, you have had the misfortune to have been broken up into various confessions and sects, so that now you have scarcely one common object of desire. But where you cannot agree among yourselves, I hope I shall be able to bring agreement to you by bestowing upon all your sects the same love and the same readiness to satisfy the *true desire* of each.

"Dear Christians! I know that for many, and not the least among you, the most precious thing in Christianity is the *spiritual authority* with which it endows its legal representatives - of course, not for their personal benefit, but for the common good, since on this authority firmly rests the true spiritual order and moral discipline so necessary for everyone. Dear brother Catholics, sister Catholics! How well I understand your view, and how much I would like to base my imperial power on the authority of your spiritual Head! In order that you should not think that this is mere flattery and windy words I, therefore, most solemnly declare that it is pleasing to our autocratic power that the Supreme Bishop of all Catholics, the Pope of Rome, be henceforth restored to his throne in Rome with all former rights and privileges belonging to this title and chair given at any time by our predecessors, from Constantine the Great onward.

"In return for this, Catholic brothers and sisters, I wish to receive from you only your inner heartfelt recognition of myself as your sole protector and patron. Let those here who recognize me in their hearts and consciences as their sole protector and patron come up to this side!"

Here he pointed to the empty seats on the platform. And instantly, nearly all the princes of the Catholic Church, cardinals and bishops, the greater part of the laypeople and over half the monks, shouting in exultation "Gratias agimus! Domine! Salvum fac magnum imperatorem[6]!" rose to the platform and, humbly bowing their heads to the Emperor, took their seats.

Below, however, in the middle of the hall, straight and immovable, like a marble statue, still in his seat sat Pope Peter II. All those who had surrounded him were now on the platform. But the diminished crowd of monks and laypeople who remained below

6 Latin, "We give thanks! Lord! Save the great emperor!"

moved nearer and closed in a dense crowd around him. And one could hear the subdued mutter issuing from them: "Non praevalebunt, non praevalebunt portae inferni[7]."

With a startled look cast at the immovable Pope, the Emperor again raised his voice: "Dear brothers and sisters! I know that there are among you many for whom the most precious thing in Christianity is its *sacred tradition* - the old symbols, the old hymns and prayers, the icons and the old rituals. What, indeed, could be more precious for a religious soul? Know, then, my beloved, that today I have signed the decree and have set aside vast sums of money for the establishment of a world museum of Christian archaeology in our glorious imperial city, Constantinople.

"This museum shall have the aim of collecting, studying, and saving all the monuments of church antiquity, more particularly Eastern church antiquity; and I ask you to select tomorrow from your midst a committee for working out with me the measures which are to be carried out, so that modern life, morals, and customs may be organized as nearly as possible in accordance with the traditions and institutions of the Holy Orthodox Church.

"My Orthodox brothers and sisters! Those of you who view with favor this will of mine, who can in their inner consciousness call me their true leader and lord, let those come up here."

Here the greater part of the hierarchy of the East and North, half of the former old believers and more than half of the Orthodox clergy, monks, and laypeople rose with joyful exclamation to the platform, casting suspicious eyes at the Catholics, who were already proudly occupying their seats.

But the Elder John remained in his place, and sighed loudly. And when the crowd round him became greatly thinned, he left his

7 Latin, "The gates of Hell will not prevail."

bench and went over to Pope Peter and his group. He was followed by the other Orthodox members who did not go to the platform.

Then the Emperor spoke again: "I am aware, dear Christians, that there are among you also such who place the greatest value upon personal assurance of the truth and the free examination of the Scriptures. There is no need for me to enlarge upon my views on this matter at the moment. Perhaps you are aware that, in my youth, I wrote a long treatise on biblical criticism which at that time excited much comment and laid the foundation for my popularity and reputation. In memory of this, I presume, the University of Tubingen only the other day requested me to accept the degree of a Doctor of Theology *honoris causa*[8]. I have replied that I accept it with pleasure and gratitude.

"And today, simultaneously with the decree of the Museum of Christian Archaeology, I signed another decree establishing a world institute for the free examination of the sacred Scriptures from all points of view and in all possible directions, and for study of all subsidiary sciences - to which institute an annual sum of one and one-half million marks is hereby granted. I call those of you who look with sincere favor upon this act of goodwill of mine and who are able in true feeling to recognize me as their sovereign leader to come up here to the new Doctor of Theology."

A strange but hardly perceptible smile passed lightly over the beautiful lips of the great man. More than half of the learned theologians moved to the platform, though somewhat slowly and hesitatingly. Everybody looked at Professor Pauli, who seemed to be rooted to his seat. He dropped his head, bent down and shrank.

The learned theologians who had already managed to get onto the platform seemed to feel very awkward, and one of them even suddenly dropped his hand in renunciation, and, having jumped right down past the stairs, ran hobbling to Professor Pauli and the

8 Latin, "For the sake of the honor."

members who remained with him. At this, the Professor raised his head, rose to his feet as if without a definite objective in view, and then walked past the empty benches, accompanied by those among his coreligionists who had also withstood the temptation. He took his seat near Elder John and Pope Peter and their followers. The greater part of the members, including nearly all the hierarchs of the East and West, were now on the platform. Below there remained only three groups of members, now coming more closely together and pressing around Elder John, Pope Peter, and Professor Pauli.

Now, in a grieved voice, the Emperor addressed them: "What else can I do for you, you strange people? What do you want from me? I cannot understand. Tell me yourselves, you Christians, deserted by the majority of your peers and leaders, condemned by popular sentiment. What is it that you value most in Christianity?"

At this, Elder John rose up like a white candle and answered quietly: "Great sovereign! What we value most in Christianity is Christ himself - in his person. All comes from him, for we know that in him dwells all fullness of the Godhead bodily. We are ready, sire, to accept any gift from you, if only we recognize the holy hand of Christ in your generosity. Our candid answer to your question, what can you do for us, is this: Confess now and before us the name of Jesus Christ, the Son of God, who came in the flesh, rose, and who will come again - Confess his name, and we will accept you with love as the true forerunner of his second glorious coming."

The Elder finished his speech and fixed his eyes on the face of the Emperor. A terrible change had come over it. A hellish storm was raging within him, like the one he experienced on that fateful night. He had completely lost his inner equilibrium, and was concentrating all his thoughts on preserving external control, so that he should not betray himself inopportunely. He was making a superhuman effort not to throw himself with wild howls on Elder John and begin tearing him with his teeth.

Suddenly, he heard a familiar, unearthly voice: "Be silent and fear not!" He remained silent. Only his face, livid like death, looked distorted and his eyes flashed. In the meantime, while Elder John was still making his speech, the great magician, wrapped in the ample tri-colored mantle that covered nearly all his cardinal's purple, could be seen busily manipulating something concealed beneath it. The magician's eyes were fixed and flashing, and his lips moved slightly. Through the open windows of the temple an immense black cloud could be seen covering the sky. Soon, complete darkness set in.

Elder John, startled and frightened, stared at the face of the silent Emperor. Suddenly, he sprang back and, turning to his followers, shouted in a stifled voice: "Little children, it is Anti-Christ!"

At this moment, a great thunderbolt flashed into the temple, followed by a deafening thunderclap. It struck the Elder John. Everyone was stupefied for a second, and when the deafened Christians came to their senses, the Elder was seen lying dead on the floor.

The Emperor, pale but calm, addressed the assembly: "You have witnessed the judgment of God. I had no wish to take any man's life, but thus my Heavenly Father avenges his beloved son. It is finished. Who will oppose the will of the Most High? Secretaries, write this down: The Ecumenical Council of All Christians, after a foolish opponent of the Divine Majesty had been struck by fire from heaven, recognized unanimously the sovereign Emperor of Rome and all the Universe as its supreme leader and lord."

Suddenly a word, loud and distinct, passed through the temple: "*Contradicatur*[9]!" Pope Peter II rose. His face flushed, his body trembling with indignation, he raised his staff in the direction of the Emperor. "Our only Lord," he cried, "is Jesus Christ, the Son of the living God! And who you are, you have heard just now. Away! You

9 Latin, "Contradicts."

Cain, you murderer! Get you gone, you incarnation of the Devil! By the authority of Christ, I, the servant of the servants of God, cast you out forever, foul dog, from the city of God, and deliver you up to your father Satan! *Anathema*[10]*! Anathema! Anathema!*"

While he was so speaking, the great magician was moving restlessly under his mantle. Louder than the last "Anathema!" the thunder rumbled, and the last Pope fell lifeless on the floor. "So die all my enemies by the arm of my Father!" cried the Emperor. "*Pereant, pereant*[11]!" exclaimed the trembling princes of the Church.

The Emperor turned and, supported by the great magician and accompanied by all his crowd, slowly walked out the door at the back of the platform. There remained in the temple only the corpses and a little knot of Christians half-dead from fear. The only person who did not lose control over himself was Professor Pauli. The general horror seemed to have raised in him all the powers of his spirit. He even changed in appearance; his countenance became noble and inspired. With determined steps, he walked up onto the platform, took one of the seats previously occupied by some State official, and began to write on a sheet of paper.

When he had finished he rose and read in a loud voice: "To the glory of our only Savior, Jesus Christ! The Ecumenical Council of our Lord's churches, meeting in Jerusalem after our most blessed brother John, representative of Christianity in the East, had exposed the arch-deceiver and enemy of God to be the true Anti-Christ foretold in Scripture; and after our most blessed father, Peter, representative of Christianity in the West, had lawfully and justly expelled him forever from the Church of God; now, before these two witnesses of Christ, murdered for the truth, this Council resolves: To cease all communion with the excommunicated one and with his

---

10 Greek, (ἀνάθεμα) “Something dedicated, especially dedicated to evil.”

11 Latin, “Confound.”

abominable assembly, and to go to the desert and wait there for the inevitable coming of our true Lord, Jesus Christ."

Enthusiasm seized the crowd, and loud exclamations could be heard on all sides. "*Adveniat! Adveniat cito! Komm, Herr Jesu, komm!* Come, Lord Jesus Christ!"

Professor Pauli wrote again and read: "Accepting unanimously this first and last deed of the last Ecumenical Council, we sign our names" - and here he invited those present to do so. All hurried to the platform and signed their names. And last on the list stood in big Gothic characters the signature: "*Duorum defunctorum testium locum tenes Ernst Pauli*[12]."

"Now let us go with our ark of the last covenant," he said, pointing to the two deceased. The corpses were put on stretchers. Slowly, singing Latin, German, and Church-Slavonic hymns, the Christians walked to the gate leading out from Haram-esh-Sheriff. Here the procession was stopped by one of the Emperor's officials who was accompanied by a squad of Guards. The soldiers remained at the entrance while the official read: "By order of his Divine Majesty. For the enlightenment of Christian people and for their protection from wicked people spreading unrest and temptation, we deem it necessary to resolve that the corpses of the two agitators, killed by heavenly fire, be publicly exhibited in the street of the Christians (Haret-en-Nasara), at the entrance into the principal temple of this religion, called the Temple of our Lord's Sepulcher, or the Temple of the Resurrection, so that all may be persuaded of the reality of their death. Their obstinate followers, who wrathfully reject all our benefits and insanely shut their eyes to the patent signs of God himself are, by our mercy and presentation before our Heavenly Father, spared a much-deserved death by heavenly fire, and are left free with the sole prohibition, necessary for the common good, of not living in towns and other inhabited places of

12 Latin, “The two deceased witnesses replace Ernst Pauli.”

residence lest they disturb and tempt innocent, simpleminded folk with their malicious inventions."

When the official had finished reading, eight soldiers, at a sign from the officer, approached the stretchers bearing the bodies. "Let what is written be fulfilled," said Professor Pauli. And the Christians who were holding the stretchers silently passed them to the soldiers, who went away with them through the northwest gate.

The Christians, having gone out through the northeast gate, hurriedly walked from the city past the Mount of Olives toward Jericho, along a road which had previously been cleared of other people by the gendarmes and two cavalry regiments. On the barren hills near Jericho, they decided to wait a few days. The following morning, friendly Christian pilgrims came from Jerusalem and told what had been going on in Zion.

After the Court dinner, all the members of the congress were invited to a vast throne hall (near the supposed site of Solomon's throne), and the Emperor, addressing the representatives of the Catholic hierarchy, told them: that the well-being of their Church clearly demanded from them the immediate election of a worthy successor to the apostate Peter; that under the circumstances the election must needs be a summary one; that his, the Emperor's, presence as the leader and representative of the whole Christian world would amply make up for the inevitable omissions in the ritual; and that he, on behalf of all Christians, suggested that the Holy College elect his beloved friend and brother Apollonius, in order that their close friendship could unite Church and State firmly and indissolubly for their mutual benefit.

The Holy College retired to a separate room for a conclave and, in an hour and a half, it returned with its new Pope, Apollonius.

In the meantime, while the election was being carried out, the Emperor was meekly, sagaciously, and eloquently persuading the

Orthodox and Evangelical representatives, in view of the new great era in Christian history, to put an end to their old dissensions, giving his word that Apollonius would be able to abolish all the abuses of the Papal authority known to history. Persuaded by this speech, the Orthodox and Protestant representatives drafted a deed of the unification of all churches, and when Apollonius appeared with the cardinals in the hall and was met by shouts of joy from all those present, a Greek bishop and an Evangelical pastor presented him with their document. "*Accipio et approbo et laetificatur cor meum*[13]," said Apollonius, signing it. "I am as much a true Orthodox and a Protestant as I am a true Catholic," he added, and exchanged friendly kisses with the Greek and the German.

Then he came up to the Emperor, who embraced him and long held him in his arms. At this time, tongues of flame began to dart about in the palace and the temple. They grew and became transformed into luminous shapes of strange beings and flowers never seen before came down from above, filling the air with an unknown perfume. Enchanting sounds of music, stirring the very depths of the soul, produced by unfamiliar instruments, were heard, while angelic voices of unseen singers sang the glory of the new lords of heaven and earth. Suddenly, a terrific subterranean noise was heard in the northwest comer of the palace under "Kubbet-el-Aruah," "the dome of souls," where, according to Muslim belief, the entrance to hell was hidden.

When the assembly, invited by the Emperor, went to that end, all could clearly hear innumerable voices, thin and penetrating - either childish or devilish - exclaiming: "The time has come, release us, dear saviors, dear saviors!" But when Apollonius, kneeling on the ground, shouted something downward in an unknown language three times, the voices died down and the subterranean noise subsided.

---

13 Latin, “I accept and approve; it brings joy to my heart.”

Meanwhile, a vast crowd of people surrounded Haram-esh-Sheriff on all sides. Darkness set in and the Emperor, with the new Pope, came out upon the eastern terrace - the signal for "a storm of rejoicing." The Emperor bowed affably on all sides, while Apollonius took magnificent fireworks, rockets, and fountains from huge baskets brought up by the cardinal deacons. Igniting them by a mere touch of his hand, he tossed them one after another into the air where they glimmered like phosphorescent pearls and sparked with all the tints of a rainbow. Reaching the ground, all the sparkles transformed into numberless variously colored sheets containing complete and absolute indulgences of all sins - past, present, and future.

Popular exultation overflowed all limits. True, there were some who stated that they had seen with their own eyes the indulgences turn into hideous frogs and snakes. But the vast majority of the people were pleased immensely, and the popular festivities continued a few days longer. The prodigies of the new Pope now surpassed all imagination, so that it would be a hopeless task even to attempt a description of them.

In the meantime, among the desert hills of Jericho, the Christians were devoting themselves to fasting and prayers. On the evening of the fourth day, Professor Pauli and nine companions, mounted on asses and taking with them a cart, stole into Jerusalem and, passing through side streets by Haram-esh-Sheriff to Haret-en-Nasara, came to the entrance to the Temple of the Resurrection, in front of which, on the pavement, the bodies of Pope Peter and Elder John were lying. The street was deserted at that time of night, as everyone had gone to Hasam-esh-Sheriff. The sentries were fast asleep.

The party that came for the bodies found them quite untouched by decomposition, not even stiff or heavy. They put them on stretchers and covered them with the cloaks they had brought with them. Then by the same circuitous route they returned to their followers. They had hardly lowered the stretcher to the ground when suddenly the spirit of life could be seen reentering the deceased bodies. The bodies moved slightly as if they were trying to throw off the cloaks in which they were wrapped. With shouts of joy, everyone lent them aid and soon both the revived men rose to their feet, safe and sound.

Then said Elder John: "Ah, my little children, we have not parted after all! I will tell you this: it is time that we carry out the last prayer of Christ for his disciples - that they should be all one, even as he himself is one with the Father. For this unity in Christ, let us honor our beloved brother Peter. Let him at last pasture the flocks of Christ. There it is, brother!" And he put his arms round Peter.

Then Professor Pauli came nearer. *"Tu est Petrus*[14]*!"* he said to the Pope, *"Jetzt ist es ja grundlich erwiesen und ausser jedem Zweifel gesetzt*[15]*."* And he shook Peter's hand firmly with his own right hand, while he stretched out his left hand to John saying: *"So also Vaterchen nun sind wir ja Eins in Christo*[16]*."*

In this manner, the unification of churches took place in the midst of a dark night on a high and deserted spot. But the nocturnal darkness was suddenly illuminated with brilliant light and a great sign appeared in the heavens; it was a woman, clothed in the sun with the moon beneath her feet and a wreath of twelve stars on her head. The apparition remained immovable for some time, and then began slowly to move in a southward direction. Pope Peter raised his staff and exclaimed: "Here is our banner! Let us follow it!" And he walked after that apparition, accompanied by both the old men and the whole crowd of Christians, to God's mountain, to Sinai ...

(Here the reader stopped.)

LADY - Well, why don't you go on?

14 Latin, "You are Peter!"

15 German, "Now it has been thoroughly proven and put beyond any doubt."

16 German, "Now, then, dear father, we are now one in Christ."

MR. Z - The manuscript stops here. Father Pansophius could not finish his story. He told me when he was already ill that he thought of completing it "as soon as I get better," he said. But he did not get better, and the end of his story is buried with him in the graveyard of the Danilov Monastery -

LADY - But you remember what he told you, don't you? Please tell us.

MR. Z - I remember it only in its main outlines. After the spiritual leaders and representatives of Christianity had departed to the Arabian desert, whither crowds of faithful believers of truth were streaming from all countries, the new Pope with his miracles and prodigies was able to corrupt unimpededly all the remaining, superficial Christians who were not yet disappointed with the Anti-Christ.

He declared that by the power of his keys he could open the gates between the earthly world and the world beyond the grave. Communion of the living with the dead, and also of the living with demons, became a matter of everyday occurrence, and new unheard-of forms of mystic lust and demonolatry began to spread among the people. However, the Emperor had scarcely begun to feel himself firmly established on religious grounds, and, having yielded to the persistent suggestions of the seductive voice of the secret "father," had hardly declared himself the sole true incarnation of the supreme Deity of the Universe, when a new trouble came upon him from a side which nobody had expected: the Jews rose against him.

This nation, whose numbers at that time had reached thirty million, was not altogether ignorant of the preparations for and the consolidation of the worldwide successes of the superman. When the Emperor transferred his residence to Jerusalem, secretly spreading among the Jews the rumor that his main object was to bring about a domination by Israel over the whole of the world, the Jews proclaimed him as their Messiah, and their exultation and devotion to him knew no bounds. But now they suddenly rose, full of wrath and thirsting for vengeance. This turn of events, doubtless foretold in both Gospel and church tradition, was pictured by Father Pansophius, perhaps, with too great a simplicity and realism.

You see, the Jews, who regarded the Emperor as a true and perfect Israelite by blood, unexpectedly discovered that he was *not even circumcised.* The same day all Jerusalem, and next day all Palestine, were up in arms against him. The boundless and fervent devotion to the savior of Israel, the promised Messiah, gave place to as boundless and as fervent a hatred of the wily deceiver, the impudent impostor. The whole of the Jewish nation rose as one man, and its enemies were surprised to see that the soul of Israel at bottom lived not by calculations and aspirations of Mammon but by the power of an all-absorbing sentiment - the hope and strength of its eternal faith in the Messiah.

The Emperor, taken by surprise at the sudden outburst, lost all self-control and issued a decree sentencing to death all insubordinate Jews and Christians. Many thousands and tens of thousands who could not arm themselves in time were ruthlessly massacred. But an army of Jews, one million strong, soon took Jerusalem and locked up the Anti-Christ in Haram-esh-Sheriff. His only support was a portion of the Guards who were not strong enough to overwhelm the masses of the enemy. Assisted by the magic art of his Pope, the Emperor succeeded in passing through the lines of his besiegers, and quickly appeared again in Syria with an innumerable army of pagans of different races. The Jews went forth to meet him with small hope of success. But hardly had the vanguard of both armies come together, when an earthquake of unprecedented violence occurred.

An enormous volcano, with a giant crater, rose up by the Dead Sea, around which the imperial army was encamped. Streams of fire flowed together into a flaming lake that swallowed up the Emperor himself, together with his numberless forces - not to mention Pope

Apollonius, who always accompanied him, and whose magic was of no avail. Meanwhile, the Jews hastened to Jerusalem in fear and trembling, calling for salvation to the God of Israel.

When the Holy City was already in sight, the heavens were rent by vivid lightning from the east to the west, and they saw Christ coming toward them in royal apparel, and with the wounds from the nails in his outstretched hands. At the same time, the company of Christians led by Peter, John, and Paul came from Sinai to Zion, and from various other parts hurried more triumphant multitudes, consisting of all the Jews and Christians who had been killed by the Anti-Christ. For a thousand years, they lived and reigned with Christ.

Here, Father Pansophius wished to end his narrative, which had for its object not a universal cataclysm of creation but the conclusion of our historical process which consists in the appearance, glorification, and destruction of the Anti-Christ.

POLITICIAN - And do you think that this conclusion is so near?

MR. Z - Well, there will be still some chatter and fuss on the stage, but the whole drama is written to the end, and neither actors nor audience will be permitted to change anything in it.

LADY - But what is the absolute meaning of this drama? I still do not understand why the Anti-Christ hates God so much, while he himself is essentially good, not evil.

MR. Z - That is the point. He is not *essentially* evil. All the meaning is in that. I take back my previous words that "You cannot explain the Anti-Christ by proverbs alone." He can be explained by a simple proverb, "All that glitters is not gold." You know all too well this glitter of counterfeit gold. Take it away and no real force remains - none.

GENERAL - But you notice, too, upon what the curtain falls in this historical drama - upon war - the meeting of two armies. So our conversation ends where it began. How does that please you, Prince? Prince? Good heaven! Where's the Prince?

POLITICIAN - Didn't you notice? He left quietly during that moving passage where the Elder John presses the Anti-Christ to the wall. I did not want to interrupt the reading at that time and, afterward, I forgot.

GENERAL - I bet he ran away - ran away a second time! He mastered himself the first time and came back, but this was too much for the poor fellow. He couldn't stand it. Dear me! Dear me!

THE END

Made in the USA
Monee, IL
16 February 2020

21856895R00026